21 DAYS TO BASIC PREPAREDNESS

SIMPLE THINGS YOU CAN DO TO PREPARE FOR ANY EMERGENCY

DAVID NASH

Copyright © 2019 by David Nash

All rights reserved.

No part of this book may be reproduced in any form or by any electronic or mechanical means, including information storage and retrieval systems, without written permission from the author, except for the use of brief quotations in a book review.

CONTENTS

Preface   v
Introduction   vii

1. Establish the Proper Mindset   1
2. Hold a Kick Off Meeting   4
3. Make a Threat Assessment   7
4. Mitigate all Threats Possible   10
5. Prioritize Your Actions   13
6. Assess Available Resources   16
7. Make a Plan   19
8. Create a Budget   22
9. Build an Important Documents Binder   24
10. Organize a 72 Hour Kit   26
11. Make a Communications Plan   29
12. Create a Plan to "Bug-Out"   31
13. Build a "Bug Out Bag"   34
14. Store Water and Learn to Purify it   36
15. Store Food and Rotate it   39
16. Consider Defensive Strategies   42
17. Don't Forget Lighting   45
18. Test Your Plan, Gear, & Yourself   47
19. Conduct an After-Action Meeting   49
20. Reassess and Repeat   51
21. Additional Resources   53

Afterword   55

PLEASE REVIEW

Bonus: Excerpt from Building a Get Home Bag   59
Also by David Nash   63
About the Author   67

PREFACE

Since you are reading a book on self-reliance, I am assuming you want to know more about how to take care of yourself in disaster situations

I would like to suggest you take a moment and visit my website and YouTube channel for thousands of hours of free content related to basic preparedness concepts

Dave's Homestead Website
https://www.tngun.com

Dave's Homestead YouTube Channel
https://www.youtube.com/tngun

Shepherd Publishing
https://www.shepherdpublish.com

INTRODUCTION

There are quite a few schools of thought when it comes to personal disaster preparedness. The largest seems to be concerned with "Stuff". I call this the government model. In this model, practitioners buy gear to solve problems. They seem to feel that money equals solutions.

While you do need to have some level of resources, I feel this is a mistake, because stuff can get stolen, damaged, or lost. If you rely solely on gear, then no matter how redundant you think you are, you still have a single point of failure.

I believe in a balanced approach. In this document, I will illustrate basic concepts for disaster preparedness as well as give you some solid tips and steps to help you begin to prepare.

There is very little in the way of gear acquisition written in the following pages. You will need to acquire some measure of food, water, and equipment if you are to become more disaster resilient, however, there are multitudes of resources on and off line to help you do just that.

What is this book is designed to do is to guide you through the first steps of personal preparedness, i.e., "getting your mind right". I find that without a solid set of guideposts, it is easy to fall down the rabbit hole and concentrate only on buying stuff, or gaining training. Both of which are necessary, but neither will allow you the flexibility to adapt, improvise, or overcome.

Venn diagram of the relationship between skills, stuff, and training

I want you to be balanced, to have the right mix of things *and* skills with a strong mindset to be able to thrive in any situation.

I do not have all the answers, but I have spent decade's figuring out the best solutions for my family. Everything I wrote here are things I have done, and it has worked well for me. Take it as a guide and a starting point, question everything, and find your own solutions.

I have taken the liberty of writing this as if we were sitting in your living room talking; it is informal because preparedness does not have to be stressful.

Please do not mistake my familiar terms for ignorance of the subject. I have a degree in Emergency Management, hold certification as Emergency Management Professional, and have over a decade in planning and teaching Emergency Management in state service as well as a lifetime of doing this with my family.

1
ESTABLISH THE PROPER MINDSET

It is no secret that I believe a proper mindset is vital to thriving in times of difficulty. In movies, Hollywood depicts typical prepper scenarios where there is no doubt that the characters are in disaster situations. In the real world however, it probably won't be so clear-cut. The popular survival concept of WROL (Without Rule of Law) is, in my opinion, a fantasy. The government has plans and procedures in provide continuity of government. What this means to you is that there may not be a clear cut signal that, "the balloon is up" and its time to change into camouflage and start carrying your AR-15s and AK-47s.

This makes mindset extremely valuable. Prepping should be integrated into your lifestyle. Preparing to surmount obstacles allows you to have a longer and better life, it is not supposed to take over your life. If being involved in prepping doesn't make your life easier, then you are doing it wrong.

Prepping is insurance for things I am either not able to fix, or cannot afford to fix on my own.

I live in the New Madrid Seismic Zone. Without a doubt, that is the largest natural threat I have. In the event we have a large-scale quake, and the infrastructure is disrupted long term, I may not be able to go to the store to buy food. That bothered me, so I took steps to learn how to grow my own food. Each new skill I learned, and each packet of seed I put back lessened my worry. I still have the Earthquake as my largest natural threat, but I am not scared of it, because I have done all I can do to be prepared for it.

Another key to the mindset of prepping is to look at your resources from an "all hazards approach". I was a prepper long before Y2K, and will be one long after 2012. I don't prep for single emergencies. I know that the seeds and food I have stored in the event of a catastrophic earthquake would also work if I lost my job, or got hurt working on some crazy project. Try to build capability and skills, rather than just work on specific threats.

Be flexible, during the Great Irish Potato Famine, only the potatoes were affected by blight, field corn, barley and oats were not. However, people starved to death while having barns full of alternative foods because they could not bring themselves to eat "horse food". I have made it a habit to look for alternative uses for products, not because it is efficient or cost effective to use things outside of their designed uses, but because it incubates mental flexibility. Historically, the ones that thrive in hard times are the quickest to adapt. - Which means - BE FLEXIBLE.

Lastly, cultivate a mindset that incorporates a tiered

approach to skill and gear acquisition. All to often, I see people that have top of the line (and expensive) equipment in one area, but nothing in other essential areas. A $6000 dollar sniper rifle and 10,000 rounds won't do you any good if you freeze to death because your electric furnace doesn't work. Make sure to be balanced. Get some food, the ability to make shelter, purify water, and defend yourself. Then get more food, and better equipment. Keep this up, and soon you will have that fancy rifle, but you will be able to stay comfortable and well fed also...

The very first step is to take a moment and think about why you are interested in prepping and what you would do to protect what you love.

2
HOLD A KICK OFF MEETING

Prepping is a lifestyle, and nothing changes lifestyle more than marriage. If you are married, or have people in your household that depend on you, then you must communicate with them.

If you do not, then you will regret it. I find that the more my wife understands about what I am doing and WHY I do it, the more she supports the direction I am leading the family in.

It is very important that after you have thought about why you want to prepare, you sit down with your loved ones and share that with them. "Honey, I love you and the kids more than anything else in life, and I worry that if something bad happened I would not be able to keep you safe. Would you help me take some steps to ensure that no matter what happens, the kids will never be cold and hungry" will make your life infinitely easier than, "Look, you just don't understand, and I don't have time to explain it, when the postman comes, just sign for the package, and put it in my office."

Get everyone's input. In the emergency management world this is called stakeholder support. If your loved ones feel like their concerns were listened to, and that they have a stake in the process, then they will most likely be more willing to sacrifice in the short term for long range results.

It is also important to get their input to ensure that you are not missing anything, that you have all the information, and that your plan is realistic.

If you ignored the mindset page, and are prepping solely for and anticipation of a commie zombie invasion that was launched after a huge solar are wiped out the national electric grid, your spouse probably won't go along with that. You should probably listen to them and compromise a little.

Go back about mindset, and look at "all hazards". A small kit to get you through a winter ice storm can serve you use in a zombie apocalypse, and it keeps the door open for upgrades over time. Failing to heed your spouse's concerns, ignoring them, and refusing to compromise ensures that each time you spend family resources on becoming more disaster resilient you are seen being in the wrong.

Involving everyone, working together, and communicating ensures that your actions are perceived in the manner they are intended, that you are a loving provider that is taking responsibility for those you love.

The more eyes on the problem, the more solutions you will

receive, and the more willing your family will be to actually practice the plan you came up with together.

Step two is to block out some time when everyone that lives in your home can sit down and discuss the idea of becoming more disaster resilient. I suggest that you share your reasoning for feeling the need to prepare, and let them share their feelings. If everyone is not on board, then do not pressure them or get offended. Being a positive role model will do much more to get them on board than badgering them will. I will say, I have experience with both models, (and one divorce...). At this point you are only opening the dialog.

Remember, prepping is not a sprint, it is a marathon. Please don't overdo it, or make it overly formal or you will probably only get frustrated and quit.

3
MAKE A THREAT ASSESSMENT

Making a threat assessment is a vital part of making a comprehensive disaster preparedness plan. If you don't know what can make you have a bad day, then you have no idea how to keep from having a bad day. Now I know that a few pages ago I made a big deal about taking an All Hazards approach to prepping, and now it may seem that I am changing midstream, but I am not.

We want out preparations to work for as many types of hazards we can, and we don't want to obsess on a single threat to the exclusions of all others.

The more we know about what can happen, the better we can focus our efforts. During this threat assessment we want to take a deeper look at anything we are worried about, as well as anything that came out of the kickoff meeting. Historical information from the local emergency management agency, and past Presidential disaster declarations (available from FEMA), also helps.

I have been trying to find a way to go to the FEMA Tsunami course they give in Hawaii, but since Tennessee is not threatened by Tsunami's I cannot justify spending any resources to prepare for that type of disaster.

Performing a threat assessment is about looking at likely threats and comparing them by how much they would impact you. This allows you to prioritize them so that you can better allocate your resources.

	Impact	Likelihood	Threat
Asteroid	10	1	5
Cuts and Scrapes	1	10	5
Home Invasion	9	3	6
New Madrid Earthquake	8	6	7
Tornado	7	5	6

A large asteroid impacting the planet would kill everyone - Impact 10, but it is unlikely, so it gets a 1 for likelihood.

I cut and burn myself regularly as I build projects, but it is rarely very serious, so impact 1, likelihood 9

This is a pretty unscientific chart, but it does a good job of showing the relationship of Impact and likelihood.

By averaging out likelihood with impacts, I can see that preparing for an earthquake or tornado is a better use of my resources than trying to figure out how to survive an asteroid impact. If I wanted to go really in depth, and make a much more useful, albeit complicated chart, I could factor in the cost to prepare, and the effectiveness of such preparations. If I did that, then asteroid impact would clearly be the least of my worries, but Home Invasion, and Tornados would both rank higher on the matrix.

Today, spend some time working on the threats that could impact your family. If you live near a highway, consider hazardous material spills, or flooding, if you live in low-lying areas.

Once you have your assessment done, you can move toward either decreasing those threats as well as preparing for them if they do occur.

4

MITIGATE ALL THREATS POSSIBLE

Once you have identified the threats that could impact your family, then the smart thing is to reduce the impact as much as possible. In emergency management mitigation is the effort to reduce loss of life and property by lessening the impact of disasters. Would you rather spend money on reducing the impact of a disaster, or fixing the damage after the fact.

I will give you an example, since earthquakes are higher on my list, I ensure that the rigid connectors (like at my water heater) are replaced with flexible connectors so that the lines won't break if shaken, and that my bookshelves are connected to the wall using nylon straps screwed to the shelf, and to a wall stud.

For home invasion, or other criminal threat, I have a plan in place, a nice alarm system, and other details that tell a criminal he would be better o trying another house.

This step will require some homework. You have to know what is likely to happen, as well as what you can do to prevent it.

I would suggest that you look into the Federal Emergency Management Agencies free independent study program. They have a course called "**IS-394.a Protecting Your Home or Small Business From Disaster**" that will explain how protective measures can reduce or eliminate long-term risks to your home and personal property from hazards.

Other resources for mitigation strategies would be your local and state emergency management agencies. I know that sometimes government grants are available for certain mitigation strategies.

After the Alabama Tornadoes of 2011, my in-laws used grant funding to have a safe room constructed at their home.

A good earthquake mitigation is installing water heater strapping

While it is a larger scope of mitigation, one of the reasons the Haiti earthquakes were so catastrophic was that local building codes were not-enforced, and the local concrete was mostly sand. The same issue of cost came into play for hurricane sandy. Flood protection is costly, so it is almost nonexistent in New York. However, the cost of the flooding dwarfs the cost of mitigation.

Mitigation is insurance, pay a little now, and hope you never have to see a benefit, or save a little now, and possibly pay a lot later.

5

PRIORITIZE YOUR ACTIONS

Hopefully your mitigation steps have lessened the impacts of disasters to the point that the list of things to do is much smaller. Once I mitigated the threat of criminal trespassers by buying an alarm, a dog, and a shotgun, I don't have to spend a lot of time worrying about it. Now I can spend my limited prepping resources on other threat types.

The next step is to take the modified risk list and look at what gives me the most bang for the buck. I can spend around $30-50 and have a pre-made 72 hour kit shipped to my door in under 15 minutes of internet shopping, or I can spend half that and go to the store and build a kit specifically designed for me. Depending on if time or money is more valuable to me.

It is very easy to achieve a minimum level of preparedness. A 72-hour kit, and some basic knowledge is the minimum recommended by FEMA and the Red Cross. A deeper level of preparedness takes more work, and it is important to know that no matter how much you spend you will never be fully prepared for every disaster.

What you need to do now is to sit back down with your spouse and look at the chart and decide if you want to go after the easiest things first, or the areas that have the most impact.

1945 Wartime Poster

Personally, I went for the easy first, both because of my all hazards ideal, and because the small wins kept the momentum going to keep my wife on board with prepping.

Something that is very important to remember when doing your prioritizing is that you are prepping because you love and cherish your family. If you spend all your time prepping, you may be neglecting them at the same time.

I have a list of things we need to buy, do, or learn to reach that next tier of preparedness, but I also know the things my wife feels are important for our family. While I am very conscious of the dollars spent, and hate to see any money wasted when it could go to preps, I also know that spending a reasonable amount of money on family entertainment isn't going to cause us to all die during the zombie apocalypse.

Personal preparedness is a balancing act. To little, and you are irresponsible, too much and your a twice divorced kook. Hitting a balance can be difficult, but it is worth it.

6
ASSESS AVAILABLE RESOURCES

The next thing to do, after you prioritize the actions you need to do to take to prepare for disasters, is to look at your resources. Typically when people hear the word *resources* they thing in terms of money or "stuff". That is part of it, but time, energy, and knowledge are also resources.

You can find ways to prepare cheaply, quickly, or effectively. You can even manage to do two of these things, but except in very rare circumstances, you are not going to be able to have all three at the same time.

One of my favorite authors is a man named **David Gingery**, his books are about making your own metal working tools, in an interview I read, Mr. Gingery spoke of how as a poor young machinist, he was often presented with problems that typically were solved with $500 solutions. Gingery said since he never had $500 he had to use his mind creatively to solve the same problem with $50. I am not a machinist, and if I tried to be I would turn a $500

Assess Available Resources

problem into a $50000 problem by wreaking the machine. What I do have is the willingness to make mistakes, and a large library of books from people who have solved similar problems. That means I can leverage other people's knowledge, and experiment and tweak to t my situation.

If I had a lot of money fall into my lap, I would use that resource to quickly buy the things I need to hit the level of preparedness I would be comfortable with, but since that is unlikely, I have to go slowly and prepare incrementally.

My wife and I have an understanding, and I know exactly how much I can spend without impacting the grocery budget. She trusts my judgment, and knows that I have an overall plan. So I am free to make the purchases we need without a lot of oversight, but to make it simple I have a list of the things we need for the current preparedness tiers and the next few tiers above that. This list contains what things cost, what is a good deal, and what price is too good to pass up.

That way, If I happen on a yard sale or somebody offers me something they don't want I can very quickly determine if its worth spending the resources on.

A full pantry is comforting, but you also need skills

Preparedness is not about buying things; true preparedness is about building capabilities. Too much stuff can be almost as bad as not enough. Most of the people killed in natural disasters like hurricanes, ignored evacuation orders so that they could stay home and protect against looters.

What you need to do is to determine how much time, money, and energy you are willing to dedicate to becoming more disaster resilient. Some weeks you will spend more, and sometimes less, but pick a number that you are comfortable with and stick to it.

7
MAKE A PLAN

You may have been wondering why this took so long to get to the planning process, but in all actuality you have been making your plan all along. You have gathered the information needed to create a concise plan that addresses exactly what you need to do.

When my "real" job was working as an emergency management planner, I spent my days writing, reviewing, and exercising state government plans for emergency response and recovery. I have used these plans numerous times in a variety of major disasters.

Let me just say, that while I believe in planning, the process used to create a plan is much more important (all this talking and thinking you had to do to get here). When the poo starts to fly, carefully crafted plans seem to follow it right out the window.

If you could plan and prepare for an event, and have everything in place and ready to go then it the event, by definition, is not a disaster. By the very nature of disaster, the things we prepare for are fluid and defy our attempts to prepare. That is why mindset, skills, and the ability to be flexible in our use of stuff are so important.

I took a firearm class once, where I was introduced to the idea that when your brain believes it is about to die it will desperately search for solutions. First it looks in its mental filing cabinet for things it has done, then things it has seen, and then things it has thought about, read about, and trained for. Since things you have done are stored visually, they the quickest things to assess. That is why you hear of someone's "life flashing before their eyes," its the ancient survival part of your brain trying to figure out how to save your life.

What the planning process does is to fill that cabinet up with ideas.

Questions you should address while writing in your plan may include:

- What constitutes a disaster?
- When should you dig out your emergency supplies?
- What would cause you to evacuate your house?
- Where would you go
- How would you get there
- What would you take with you?
- What sorts of medications do you need to store?
- If you have defensive concerns; what would cause me to take a life?

- What happens if an emergency occurs during the week and no one is home?
- How would you get water, food, and power during an extended emergency?
- How would you deal with sanitation during an extended period without infrastructure?
- How tightly do you want to hold the information that you have some level of preparedness?
- How would you deal with hungry neighbors that did not prepare?
- How much do you need to store
- How will you fit it all in your home?

These questions are endless, and it seems the more I answer the more questions I find to answer. It is your plan, and it is based upon your lifestyle and needs. Don't over-complicate it, but the deeper you go the better your plan will be.

CREATE A BUDGET

Now that you know what you are planning for, what need, what you have, and how much you can spend to make those two the same. Now what you need to do is write it down into a prepper budget.

I don't get overly complicated in mine (the wife rolls her eyes at that), I just have a monthly goals I want to accomplish. This month's goal may be to buy "X" dollars of bulk food, build something, or read so many books.

Without written goals I tend to procrastinate or waste resources on pet projects that really aren't all that effective. I see this quite often with new preppers, and I did it myself. We tend to focus on really neat ideas that really aren't effective or efficient uses of our time.

These goals are time based and lead down a clear path in the direction of where I want to be.

Your goals and mine are different. I am more into **prepsteading**, and don't feel that I will ever be prepared enough until I have some acreage and the ability to grow my own crops. For almost everyone else a year's supply of food is probably more than enough.

No matter who you are, and where you want to take your desire to be more prepared for disaster, please realize that it takes action on your part. You have to get out and do it.

Writing down time based goals that complement your written plan and fit within the resource allocations you have previously made is an essential part of the process.

In the end it is all about how you manage time, money, and effort is the attempt to meet your goals.

9
BUILD AN IMPORTANT DOCUMENTS BINDER

I believe that prepping is a lifestyle, and that the actions you take to prepare for disaster ought to make your life easier. For the beginning prepper, nothing illustrates this more than an emergency document binder.

All this binder does is organize and store your vital identity documents and other paperwork. If you buy a sturdy binder and some clear plastic sheet protectors and business card sheets you can collect your birth certificates, social security cards, insurance paperwork, licenses, marriage and divorce documentation, voter registration, mortgage paperwork, and whatever other documents that you may need at a moment's notice.

This makes your day to day life easier, as you don't have to search for records when you need them, but in a situation where you have to leave quickly having everything in one place is the difference between the relief of having the documents you need with you and having added the stress of having to replace everything.

As with all things prepping, you can go as deep with this as you want. I found DVD sleeves that attach to binders with adhesive, and have begun putting DVD copies of my course material in my training binders. I can see the benefit of putting PDF copies of your documents, scans of your medical records, and digital copies of your irreplaceable family photos.

Keeping your important documents together is just good common sense

While working with evacuees for hurricane Katrina and Gustav, it came to my attention that many in the shelters did not have their identity documents because they were lost during the storm and resulting chaos. While case manager's helped them replace the paperwork. I am sure that the citizen's did not need the extra difficulty of having to do that.

Prepping should make life easier, and this binder is the first step of realizing that.

10

ORGANIZE A 72 HOUR KIT

Every website on disaster preparedness, from Government website like **FEMA** and **Ready.gov**, to nongovernmental websites like the **Red Cross**, or prepper sites like **mine**, has a section on organizing a 72 hour kit.

The reason for this is simple, if you can take care of yourself for three days without needing outside assistance, you can weather the vast majority of situations. For large-scale disasters, it will take at least three days for the governmental response agencies to get their systems activated and in place.

During the Nashville floods of 2010, the State of Tennessee began ordering vital supplies immediately, but it took time to load the trucks and drive them in from neighboring states. Everything then need to be o loaded and sent to points of distribution to be given to needed citizens. In large-scale disasters, local responders might also be victims themselves.

It is just common sense to take such universal advice. So what should you put in your kit?

An example of a small 72-hour kit

Obviously you need 72 hours' worth of food and water, but what kind and how much. Personally, I don't use military based MREs for my long term food storage. They are too expensive, have too short of a shelf life, and when I was in the Marines I ate my ll of them. However, the convenience of them outweighs the negatives for short-term kits. They are very portable and contain enough calories that 2 MREs a day can keep you going. That means a $60 pack of 12 meals would last a family of 4 for 3 days.

Add the recommended 1 gallon a day per person allowance of water, and a 6 gallon water tote makes up a great start.

I have a pair of spare eyeglasses and prescription medicine in my kit, as well as some wool blankets, a non-electric can opener, lots of garbage bags, flashlights, batteries, and anything else I would need to get my family through three long days.

A NEW PACK OF CARDS, a Hoyle card game rulebook, and some coloring books are also vital to your sanity. The iPods probably won't have juice enough to last through a minor disaster, and kids need to have something to do to prevent meltdowns.

This isn't a pack it and forget it kit, you need to check the contents a couple times a year and rotate the food and batteries.

If you never check it, then the odds are that the gear will be broken, missing, or expired when it is time to actually use it.

11

MAKE A COMMUNICATIONS PLAN

We are a society that is built upon our communications infrastructure. We commute long distances to work, and rely very heavily on our cellular phones to conduct business.

Since our networks are built in response to demand, it is very easy to overtax the system. If you have ever noticed that you get more dropped cell calls during rush hour you can easily extrapolate that during crisis it is very likely that cell service will be inoperable.

However, that is not the only means to communicate. If you have a cell phone and can send SMS text messages, you may have better luck with them because texts use less data than a voice call, and your phone can hold it until it can find enough available bandwidth to get the message out.

Also, certain phone companies have mentioned that due to the way the system is designed calls outside of affected areas can get through when calls within disaster areas are blocked.

During the Alabama tornadoes of 2011, I was able to use my cell phone to call my wife's family and pass messages back and forth when they could not call each other directly even though they were only a few miles apart.

Having a communications plan is more than deciding to become a ham radio operator (even though that is a good idea, and not as hard as many think).

Part of a communications plan is bout about actions like establishing an out of state contact person that can relay messages, and partly about learning what you can do to communicate during a disaster.

An example might be that you and your wife both commute to work, and your jobs and your home are in three separate counties. If you have a large disaster during the workweek, and you cannot communicate via normal channels, you will both head home. You may decide that if your wife does not come home within a specified time frame you will go to her, and that she could leave a special mark on her route to designate she took an alternate route so you do not search in the wrong area.

This could also be a nonverbal signal that you can use in public to signal danger. In my firearm classes we go over the idea that you really don't want to be in a gunfight, but you REALLY don't want to be in one with the wife walking next to hugged up on your dominant hand. Maybe a signal to take the kids and "go away" might be worth talking about...

12

CREATE A PLAN TO "BUG-OUT"

In the disaster preparedness world, there are a few main schools of thought about "bugging out," some do it as a first resort, others as a last resort, and some live full time at their bug-out locations because they already own a homestead.

I don't have any hard and fast rules about bugging out or hunkering down. I personally feel that as long as it is safe to do so, I would rather stay at home because I have a lot more resources at home than I can carry on my back. Besides that, once you leave your home during a disaster, you may not be able to come back; you also may not be able to get to where you were planning to go.

However, my house is not my primary focus, and all the stuff in it is only there for the benefit of my family. If the situation called for leaving, I would leave in a heartbeat. I would not want to disregard an evacuation order and hope a National Guard helicopter would rescue us from the top of our roof.

However, I don't want to leave the relative security of my home without a plan.

When I step up my long-term food storage, I do so in a way that my food is split up into functional areas. Instead of packing one 5 gallon bucket full of wheat, I take that same bucket and put smaller bags in it, so that I would have 2 gallons of wheat, one of salt, sugar, and beans. That way if I had to leave and did not have the time to sort through buckets I could grab a couple and not have to worry about accidentally grabbing a bucket of baking powder, and another of salt.

I also have some large plastic bins that have the basic function marked on them with colored duct tape. Red is medical, green is camping supplies, white is defensive items, and blue is food. I don't have to waste time searching for stuff; I can just fill the truck up with one each if I only had a few minutes to prepare to leave.

Color coding gear makes it much easier to find

Not only does your plan need to address what to take, but also it needs to cover where to go and how to get there. I hate it when non-preppers tell me they are coming to my house in the event of a disaster, and I am touchy about doing that to my friends. I have agreements with a few close friends and family that I can go to their house, and they can come to mine in the event of a disaster. Some are local, others regional, and a few are out of state.

I have looked at maps to find alternative routes to their homes, and when time is available I try to run those routes in advance and look for places to rest and refuel on the way.

The last thing I can tell you about bugging out is, that if you think you may have to, it is best to be the first one out. If you wait too long, you may find the road is impassable.

13
BUILD A "BUG OUT BAG"

A bug out bag is not the same as a 72-hour kit; it can be larger if designed for a car, or smaller if it designed to be used as a backpack. I have tried both over the years and have compromised to find a solution that works best for me.

What I did was stock more items in a large plastic tote, and include a backpack. I keep this kit in my car and if I should ever have to walk home or had to leave the house with no notice I can pick and choose from the car kit and put the items in the backpack.

Alternatively, if you did not want to fill up your car with a kit, you could build a kit around a backpack and keep it stored somewhere in your home that is easy to access, but out of the way. It would be nice if it was not hidden away so that you forget to rotate your food and expendable gear, but if it is too accessible, I find that it becomes an easy place to raid for batteries when the TV remote dies, or the kid wants a granola bar.

I will caution you about the outward appearance of your kit. As I watch YouTube and visit prepper related sites, I see a lot of folks with military looking gear. I would not be very accommodating if, during a large-scale disaster, a couple armed men with chest rigs and camouflage packs strolled through my yard. (However, it is pretty normal here where I live.)

Depending on the situation, I can see several bad endings, from arrest to being killed for your stuff.

My pack is a beat up looking, but is in good condition. It is a nice and dirty looking dark blue. If the situation called for it, and I choose to carry a gun in the kit, it would probably not be a military caliber rifle. I think they have a definite place in disaster preparations, but in most of the situations I can think of that have a realistic chance of occurring, it is my opinion that they bring too much negative attention for the benefits they bring. (For bugging out and walking down the road that is.)

Remember, the military uses firepower for suppression, and are just a radio call from resupply.

If you have ever tried carrying 300 rounds of ammo and a rifle in addition to your kit, you will find that it cuts down on maneuverability. However, a nice sized handgun, concealed about your person, while looking non-threatening but alert, and without any ostentatious gear screaming, "Rob Me!" may be a better solution.

It is not about looking cool, or feeling like John Wayne, it is about getting to safety as quickly and efficiently as possible.

14

STORE WATER AND LEARN TO PURIFY IT

Earlier, when discussing 72-hour kits I mentioned that the standard amount of water recommended is one gallon per person per day. This is a universal recommendation, but depending on time of year, climate, and if you want to stay clean, it is not enough. However, when balancing the weight and size of water, with its universal use, one gallon a day is a good compromise.

We store water in a variety of ways both for utility, for redundancy, and for convenience. Our main method of storing water is to use plastic 5-gallon jerry cans. They used to sell these at Wal-Mart for around $10, but I haven't seen one there in 10 years. I have seen them at sporting good stores for $20, and I have a standing order with the wife to buy any she sees, whenever she finds them if they are $20 or less.

Right now I keep 5 full of water next to the washer in out basement. I consider that a 4 day supply for the kid, my

Store Water and Learn to Purify it

wife, and I. That gives me some extra to take care of hygiene.

I also try to take clear 2 liter soda bottles, and after cleaning out the soda, refill them, and freeze them in our deep freezer. The machine is more efficient when full, and if the power is out for a short time, the ice acts to moderate the temperature.

Whatever method of storage you use, make sure you add a little chlorine to the bottle to kill any pathogens.

Use non-scented chlorine bleach, and only add a few drops per gallon. The chlorine will dissipate over time, but if sealed tightly, no bacteria can get in.

Like food, you cannot store enough water to survive long term;

You need to have a method to get water if the electricity is down. I keep extra food grade buckets to transfer water from a nearby creek.

I also have several methods of purifying the water. Boiling works well, but it takes a lot of energy, filters also work well, and I have several but they may not filter out all the pathogens. I have a bulk container of chorine based powder pool-shock that I can use to make a bleach solution to add to the water to kill bacteria.

This is one area where you cannot skimp, water purification methods are too cheap, too plentiful, and the risks from drinking unsafe water too great to risk not taking the extra step.

Water borne diarrhea is uncomfortable during normal

times, but is a major cause of death in countries without infrastructure, in crisis, or otherwise lacking medical facilities.

15

STORE FOOD AND ROTATE IT

With the exception of rearms, nothing in the world of personal preparedness has as many differing viewpoints of what is "the right way" as food storage. What to store, how much to store, and how to store the food are all things you will have to decide for yourself. There are a few different routes you can take based upon your resources and concerns.

The first thing you have to decide is what your target amount of food to store is. 3 days of food for your family is the universally recommended starting point, but consider how short a time that is. There have been many winter storms that have impacted communities for twice or three times the 72-hour number. A pandemic u could have an incubation period of a week, and to prevent exposure you may have to stay sheltered in your home for 10 or more days.

We have a target of one year for the three people in my household. However, I have several family members who may come to my house during a disaster. If that occurs, my 3 person year supply turns to a 6 month supply with 6 people, or much shorter supply if my parents come and my sister brings her 6 kids.

Once you decide on a target amount, you need to decide are you going to pack the food yourself or are you going to buy it commercially. I have bought 50# bags of wheat for under $15, but a 44# bucket of wheat packaged for storage can cost $50.00. Time is valuable, and there is a learning curve to packing your own, but the cost savings can be tremendous.

What types of food to store is also a decision point. We use the LDS guidelines of 400 pounds of grain, 60 pounds of beans, 16 pounds milk (triple if you have kids), 10 quarts cooking oil, 60 pounds sugar or honey, and 8 pounds salt per person.

This will keep you alive, is cheap, and when packed and stored properly it can last a lifetime. However it is not the most fun diet in the world.

To help with food fatigue, we augmenting it with foods we NORMALLY eat. This adds variety as well as keep incorporate our food storage into our daily life to both adjust our bodies to the food, and to learn how to cook it in enjoyable ways. You can buy freeze dried bulk food also, and I recommend doing so if your budget allows. It stores well, gives variety to your meals, and tastes much better than sprouted wheat and powdered milk. Unfortunately it is much more expensive, and many of the prepackaged deals that advertise a certain amount of calories per day pad their numbers with a lot of wheat at inflated costs.

MRE's and other shelf stable convenience meals are also useful, but they don't last as long, are more bulky, and cost the most of any of the other options. However, for short-term disasters the convenience offered can offset the negative aspects.

The key is to test the items you store so you pick things that you will eat and enjoy, and then incorporate these items into your daily life so that you are eating what you store, and storing what you eat, this helps keep your inventory fresh, as well as keeping your body from having a huge shock due to a change in diet.

16

CONSIDER DEFENSIVE STRATEGIES

The most controversial subject in prepping has to be guns. I am not going to get into the politics of gun ownership, and this is too short a space to delve too deep into training. There are three things I want to emphasize that are vitally important to a prepper.

There are "preppers" (and you may be one of them), that foresees a coming disaster that will be catastrophic, and they choose to prepare for it. However, these "preppers" chose to prepare in one solitary aspect. They buy guns.

If your disaster preparedness plans are all about guns and have nothing about food, you are not prepping, you are planning to murder people for their food.

You are saying when the "shit hits the fan" you are going to go out and steal from people who have food. If you go the opposite route and have no defensive tools then you are planning to become a victim.

Guns are tools, and not objects of worship. I like guns, I

Consider Defensive Strategies

like that they represent equality and freedom, and I enjoy shooting them, but I don't buy them for looks, or to be cool. I buy rearms with a proven track record in common calibers. My collection won't impress my friends, and are not the newest gun featured in a magazine, but they go bang every time I pull the trigger, and shoot calibers that are common enough to be found in any sporting goods store.

Owning a gun does not mean you know to use it effectively. Shooting is a skill, not a gift. You have to practice and you have to have some degree of academic knowledge.

You do not have to spend a fortune and go to fancy shooting schools, but proper training from a skilled instructor is well worth the effort.

Get the best you can afford

As a firearm instructor I have seen the difference quality makes when it comes to guns and accessories. I know that everyone cannot afford a new gun, and that any gun is better than no gun. But when students come to a class and have an extremely inexpensive gun that has not been properly taken care of, a gun that malfunctions often rewards them for their choices.

Nothing is louder than a click when you need a bang. On the other side of the coin, I see students bring in very expensive guns and try to shoot cheap bullets and carry the gun on a cheap belt in a cheaper holster. They spend an inordinate amount of time fumbling around with an uncomfortable setup.

As a new prepper, if you are serious about wanting to own a gun, I would take some simple steps. First I would take a basic class. The NRA, or a state carry permit class (if available) are perfect class choices for new shooters.

Then I would find a range that rents guns and shoot several different types of guns to get a feel for what you think is comfortable. I would then buy a gun, bullets, and if a pistol a holster and belt, that are good enough quality that you can afford them, but is expensive enough that you feel it.

You need something that is quality so that it is reliable, large enough so that it moderates the recoil of the cartridge, and the largest cartridge you are comfortable with.

Gun ownership is a personal issue, and I am hesitant to recommend a particular model over another without knowing a person's circumstances, but a decent pistol in 9mm, .38, .40, or .45 works well, as do shotguns in 12 or 20 gauge, and rifles in common calibers such as .223, .308, or 30-06.

17

DON'T FORGET LIGHTING

In most disasters that someone could reasonably plan for, it is a good assumption that the power grid will be down. Electrical power can be an issue, but once you realize that electrical power is relatively new and that people have survived thousands of years without it, you should realize that you could survive without it also.

That being said, the things that electricity powers are important, and lighting is something you definitely need to be prepared. If you cannot find your circuit breaker in the dark because you don't have batteries in your flashlight then you are a very poor prepper. Like all things related to preparedness, we follow the tiered approach, and are as redundant as possible.

I have a habit of buying small led flashlights and hanging them on the backs of bedroom doorknobs. They are out of the way, very handy, and by being inside of bedrooms; they do not interfere with my wife's decorating scheme. The LED flashlights are very handy, and do not take a lot of power to work, so a stockpile of AA batteries can last a long time.

We keep a high-intensity "tactical" light in the bedroom, as well as a lower power, but more efficient D-cell mag-light.

I have several camping lanterns, fuel, and mantles in my camping boxes, as well as old style kerosene lamps and lots of candles. However, if you are going to rely on flammable lighting, matches, wicks, fuel, fire protection, and smoke and CO alarms are mandatory to store also.

simple mason jar oil lamp

I have learned how to make my own candles and make simple lamps from **mason jars**, cotton strung, wire, and old olive oil. Simply bend a wire (or paperclip) to hold a bit of cotton string right at the surface level of oil in a jar. The cotton will wick up the oil and burn with little smoke and is relatively bright.

However, since the majority of our lighting comes from flashlights, we store lots of batteries. I prefer rechargeable batteries, and have a small solar charger. They are more expensive, but are more economical with use.

18

TEST YOUR PLAN, GEAR, & YOURSELF

I commend you for recognizing the need to become more prepared, and if you have taken the steps to get you to this point you now have a plan of action as well as the basic ability to support yourself with food, water, light, and keep people from stealing your food water and light the next thing to do is to test your plan.

Without actually testing your plan you have no idea that it can work, not only that, but by testing it you push your prepping skills higher up that mental toolbox so that if you are ever unexpectedly thrown into disaster your mind has a stronger frame of reference. That will allow you to better manage the stress as well as to react quicker.

There is a science to exercising plans, you don't go all out and kill your electricity and try to survive for a month the first time out. Professional emergency managers work up to full-scale exercises by first having what is known as a table top.

In a tabletop exercise, all the key players sit down at a table and are presented with a problem. For example, a tornado came through town and your home was not destroyed, but the roof was damaged, and power is out. Each player will then say what they would do based upon what they have, not what they want. The key is to only use skills, knowledge, and equipment you have available. This will help identify what else you need.

A family camping trip is also a great way to test a 72-hour or bug out kit

Once you have done that, pick a weekend when everyone is home, and commit to having a trial run without using your utilities. That means no electricity, no heat or cooling, and no running water.

Use only what you have at your house, and set up a schedule so that someone is always awake during the night to be on " fire watch".

It's not particularly fun, but it is an invaluable training tool to help you realize that you can survive hardship, as well as help you gain experience in what works and what does not.

19
CONDUCT AN AFTER-ACTION MEETING

Immediately after an exercise, professional responders frequently have what is known as a "hot wash" or after action briefing. No matter what you call it, this gives emergency personnel the opportunity to discuss what works, what doesn't and how to improve.

It is vital that you do this at the end of your weekend exercise before everyone gets back on their iPad and returns to normal life.

Make sure that no matter what happened in your trial run, the discussion stays positive. If junior snuck in the kitchen and ate all the survival cookies, don't say,"junior ate all the cookies". Point out that maybe you need to focus on storing more food because your allotment isn't enough to satisfy, or that the fire-watch needs to be more than one person. Maybe the solution is to put a lock on the cookies? Remember the reason for an after action review it to look for solutions to problems, not people to blame.

You do not have to make this extremely formal, and it should not take a long time. However, if you wait to do it, chances are you will keep putting it off and valuable lessons will be lost.

Additionally, by planning, having a table top, having a functional exercise, and then critiquing it afterwards your brain will be "tricked" into thinking it has been involved in that type of action several times, so that if the time comes it will seem much more normal to your subconscious. That will allow you to get up to speed much more quickly.

20

REASSESS AND REPEAT

After your hot wash, both the after-action brief, and the long shower you will enjoy after the weekend with no power, begin the process of taking what you have learned and reassess you plan. What you have learned will give you insight into making a better plan. Emergency management is a cyclical discipline, and professional emergency planners are always planning, training, testing, and planning some more.

Emergency Preparedness Cycle

Each cycle gets you more prepared for disasters, teaches your family to work as a group, and increases your comfort level.

Depending on your situation, what you are preparing for, and your level of comfort you can take this as seriously as you want. But, a single rotation of the preparedness cycle is a vast improvement over the general population.

If you keep the cycle going, and are creative in your exercises, (say exploring alternate routes of travel during a weekend getaway) you can make this a fun part of your lifestyle.

We like to take classes, and spend our time building and creating new things that make us more prepared and self-reliant, but that's because we enjoy doing it.

We prepare because we love out family, lets make it a family activity

Prepping should not be a chore; it should be a path that balances your life. Your take extra effort in easy times so you will make tough times easier.

21
ADDITIONAL RESOURCES

I wanted to keep this document short and as an easy first steps guide, but if you are interested in learning more, I have included links to free articles from my site that are related to the concepts you have read about here:

- **Why Have a Personal Preparedness Mindset**
- **Why We Prepare**
- **Dealing with Family that Doesn't Understand Emergency Preparedness**
- **$10 Weekly Food Storage Program**
- **Introduction to Emergency Kits**
- **Bulk Food Storage Using Mylar Bags**
- **Water Storage**
- **DIY Bucket Water Filter**
- **Pool Shock for Water Purification**
- **Firearm Safety**

- **Firearms for Catastrophic Disasters**
- **Should You Shoot to Wound or to Kill?**
- **Communications Plan**

AFTERWORD

If prepping makes your life difficult, then you are not doing it right.

Prepping is life insurance, it is common sense, and it should make you sleep easier at night.

I sincerely hope you have learned something from this small booklet, and that it has given you information that will cause you to take longer steps down the road to a more self-reliant lifestyle.

PLEASE REVIEW

Please visit my Amazon Author Page at:

https://amazon.com/author/davidnash

if you like my work, you can really help me by publishing a review on Amazon.

The link to review this work at Amazon is:

https://www.amazon.com/review/create-review?asin=B07BPHHL8T

BONUS: EXCERPT FROM BUILDING A GET HOME BAG

A bugout bag/72 hour kit is one of the very first projects a new prepper makes as they explore the idea of becoming more self-reliant. A quick search for the term "bug out bag" on Amazon kindle shows more than 9 pages of books. Why should you read this one?

I can only explain why by telling you my own personal ideas on the subject. With very few exceptions, the "experts" in prepping are all just selling you their own ideas and personal bias. Most of us teach what we believe, but are not a lot of writers in this subject that have lived through a grid down or other catastrophic disaster, so as I said, its all personal ideas.

While it is true that I haven't lived through a Zombie Apocalypse, I have a unique set of skills. I have been a personal preparedness advocate since I led a school-wide new Madrid preparation program as a High School Freshman. After the Marines, and a few years working inside various state prisons, I began working in state level emergency management. I have a degree in Emergency Management, and worked for over a decade in preparedness planning, training, and operations at the State level. I know exactly how the government will react and what they are prepared to do. I also understand the prepper mindset, as I have been one since junior high school.

This book is similar in scope to my 21 Days to Basic Preparedness ebook in that it explores personal preparations from the viewpoint of the modern science of emergency management. In this short work I will discuss the fundamental differences in types of emergency kits and bags. However, this work focuses on the specifics of a Get Home Bag rather than a more general bug out bag. I also hope to help you build a kit that will actually be useful rather than something that may get you in trouble or be too heavy to carry.

I have worked in emergency management during some very serious disasters. I was in charge of the Logistical Support Area for the May 2010 Nashville Floods, worked support during Katrina, and during my time in Operations I participated in hundreds of smaller scale local disasters and emergency response activities. I have even worked a nuclear plant emergency response once or twice. From that experience, I know the work and thought that goes into running a shelter during a disaster. Emergency management workers try very hard to make shelters safe and comfortable. However, the lack of privacy, resources, and independence makes me pretty hesitant to choose to go to a shelter as long as I have other options.

Personally, it would take a very severe reason for me to evacuate or "bug out" from my home in the first place. Leaving the house would entail me having to leave many of my in-place systems and make me more vulnerable to outlaws and well meaning (and otherwise) bureaucrats.

However, just because I don't WANT to evacuate from my homestead doesn't mean I won't HAVE to evacuate. I don't want any kind of disaster to befall my family, but measuring risk says I should be prepared "just in case".

While, my goal is to not have to bug out, I can see lots of situations where I would need to "get home"

Before we get into the necessity to have a special kit in your vehicle that will help you "get home". There is a need to discuss the various types of emergency kits. However, buying a bag of stuff won't help if you don't have the skills and mindset to use them. In my experience, both as a prepper, and an emergency manager, I find that before you should buy things you should develop the right skills.

If you like this Introduction to Building a Get Home Bag, you can find it on Amazon.

ALSO BY DAVID NASH

Fiction

The Deserter: Legion Chronicles Book 1
The Revolution: Legion Chronicles Book 2
The Return: Legion Chronicles Book 3
The Warrior: Legion Chronicles Book 4

Homestead Basics

The Basics of Raising Backyard Chickens
The Basics of Raising Backyard Rabbits
The Basics of Beginning Beekeeping
The Basics of Making Homemade Cheese
The Basics of Making Homemade Wine and Vinegar
The Basics of Making Homemade Cleaning Supplies
The Basics of Baking
The Basics of Food Preservation
The Basics of Food Storage
The Basics of Cooking Meat
The Basics of Make Ahead Mixes
The Basics of Beginning Leatherwork

Non Fiction

21 Days to Basic Preparedness

52 Prepper Projects

52 Prepper Projects for Parents and Kids

52 Unique Techniques for Stocking Food for Preppers

Basic Survival: A Beginner's Guide

Building a Get Home Bag

Handguns for Self Defense

How I Built a Ferrocement "Boulder Bunker"

New Instructor Survival Guide

The Prepper's Guide to Foraging

The Prepper's Guide to Foraging: Revised 2nd Edition

The Ultimate Guide to Pepper Spray

Understanding the Use of Handguns for Self Defense

Note and Record Books

Correction Officer's Notebook

Get Healthy Notebook

Rabbitry Records

Collections and Box Sets

Preparedness Collection

Legion Chronicles Trilogy

Translations

La Guía Definitiva Para El Spray De Pimienta

Multimedia

Alternative Energy
Firearm Manuals
Military Manuals 2 Disk Set

ABOUT THE AUTHOR

 David Nash is a former Marine with over a decade of experience in Emergency Management and another ten years in Corrections. He currently works in training as an instructor at a correction academy teaching new officers how to handle angry felons.

Add in a couple of semesters working in a liquor store during college and he has seen it all. In fact, David had the third highest prepper score on the NatGeo show Doomsday Preppers as well as worked more than 20 Presidentially declared disasters.

He has authored several books on preparedness, as well as worked on several disaster response plans as a state planner.

He is a father and a husband. He enjoys time with his young son William Tell and his school teacher wife Genny. When not working, writing, creating content for YouTube, playing on his self-reliance blog, or smoking award-winning BBQ he is asleep.

- amazon.com/author/davidnash
- facebook.com/booksbynash
- youtube.com//tngun
- goodreads.com/david_allen_nash
- twitter.com/dnash1974
- instagram.com/shepherdschool
- pinterest.com/tngun

Made in the USA
Coppell, TX
11 April 2024

31132240R10049